Best Wishes

Jerry Kelley

Reaching For Manhood
At Steamboat Bay

Recollections of a boy's adventures in Southeastern Alaska

Summer 1939

Jerry Kelley

A Lighthouse Press Publication
division of **ProStar** *Publications*, Inc.

ISBN: 1-57785-548-5
Printed in the USA

Published by:

Lighthouse Press

a division of **ProStar** Publications, Inc

3 Church Circle, Suite 109
Annapolis, MD 21401

(800) 481-6277

Email: orders@prostarpublications.com
www.prostarpublications.com

To Vivian

This little book is dedicated to my wife, partner and best friend for the last fifty-five years. She inspires, praises, comforts me, goads and cajoles me. In her incisive critique of my writings no hold is barred, including hugs. As disease has distorted my central vision she has typed from my trembling handwritten manuscripts, then helped me cope with the computer as I shifted to that medium. She transports me wherever I go, not withstanding my unwelcome assistance with her driving.

She is always honest. She loves me. Though she steers us across the matrimonial seas no fathometer can read the depth of my admiration and love for her.

ACKNOWLEDGEMENTS

Family: In addition to the major contribution by my wife, Vivian, our sons Mark and Michael, and their wives Kim and Kathy, were consistent boosters and advisors. Also, Vivian's ninety-nine year old mother, Marion Hixon, unfailingly asked, "How's your book coming? " Her cogent mind still induces a modicum of guilt.

Friends: However, the master of the guilt genre was my neighbor and dear friend, Gordon Prichard. For years he nagged me to write. Now he asks, "What's your next topic?" Oh yes, I'm also indebted to him for computer help, as are both Jack and Mary Jane Kutz who were troubleshooters with my word processing woes. My four English teacher friends, Mary Lou (Rude) Leidheiser, Mary Lelewer, Barb Masterson and Donna Prichard (nagger Gordon's wife), critiqued and encouraged me.

Colleagues: Immeasurable thanks to the members of the "Writer's Tune-up" group, which I joined with great trepidation, several years ago, bringing only a handful of poems. These gifted knowledgeable writers took in this elderly, legally blind novice, and educated, critiqued and occasionally even applauded him. The group's leader, Colleen W. Cain, was particularly influential. She supportively edited my work, and helped me prepare it for possible publication.

Resource people: These are vision professionals who facilitated better use, including writing, of my remaining sight. Carin Mack was the coordinator of a low vision support group, from whom I learned of the blinded veteran's program at the V.A. Hospital, American Lake, Washington. The ever ebullient Ellen Martin cleared the way for my admission to the rehabilitation clinic, where I was a resident for six weeks. All the staff at the clinic worked a magic that left each of us better equipped and more optimistic about our futures with visual handicaps. Finally, James McMillan, M.D., ophthalmologist extraordinaire. Even though my macular degeneration is a progressive disease, I have suffered no further sight loss in my three years under his care.

Special thanks to illustrator Richard Myers. His excellent drawings were completed within a two-day time window after he first read the script.

All of the above persons contributed to the completion of this little book, whether they knew it or not.

FOREWORD

Life was simple then. Families had clung together during the great depression. We amused ourselves with card games and Monopoly. We sat around the radio Saturday night for 'One Man's Family', and 'I Love a Mystery'. On Sunday we heard 'Jack Benny', 'Burns and Allen', and (banjo eyes) 'Eddie Cantor'. Movies were wholesome. Even married couples were never seen in bed together. No TV, no drugs, no gangs, no drive-in theaters, no bikinis, no Elvis. Life was happy, but unexciting. I had traveled only as far as Coeur d' Alene, Idaho, and that when we lived right across the border, in Spokane, Washington. After moving to Seattle in 1929, we occasionally visited other places in our state, but were usually home in West Seattle. During those ten years until I finished high school, I was mostly just trying to grow up. In an age of innocents, I was among the most.

But, as the flowers opened up in the spring of 1939, so did my prospects. I could hardly wait for summer. Thanks to my next-door neighbor, Harold E. "Jack" Dempsey, I was to be a deckhand on boats and fish traps, for the New England Fish Company salmon cannery, at Steamboat Bay, Noyes Island, Alaska.

I jumped at the chance for instant manhood, a

daunting leap for this barely seventeen-year old under-sized boy of 125 pounds. This book tells my impression-istic memoir of that time sixty-five years earlier.

All of the events, anecdotes and stories are essen-tially factual. Most of the names are genuine, but each name represents a real person. However, the absence of tangible souvenirs, other than a handful of faded photo-graphs, results in less exact specifics. Such factors as dimensions, distances, weather details and bits of dia-logue represent my best estimates these decades later. Everything flows from, and is consistent with, those images, still fresh and vivid in my mind. Those experi-ences were central in my development into a confident adult male.

SYNOPSIS

CHAPTER ONE: **Go North, Young Man.** On his own for the first time, an adolescent boy heads to Alaska on a steamship. He's on his way to his first job, for a salmon cannery at remote Steamboat Bay, Noyes Island. He gets crushes on two attractive older girls on board, but fails to find the nerve to become affectionate. He says goodbye in Ketchikan, and hustles to board the cannery boat *Cape Ulitka*, headed for Steamboat Bay.

CHAPTER TWO: **Puttin' on the Cape.** He meets the very interesting three-man crew of the boat, and gets his first lessons in deck work, seamanship, and navigation, while making the slow trip to Noyes Island. All new, all exciting, and only the prelude to six weeks of adventure. Can he handle what lies ahead?

CHAPTER THREE: **The Noyes Makers**. With disbelieving eyes the spurt-growing boy consumes the first of many huge feasts in the mess hall, and also tastes the hard work in the warehouse.Then he begins an acquaintance with the other residents of the bunkhouse, the highly skilled men who actually run the cannery. They are all old enough to be his father, some his grandfather. Can he fit in? He survives their teasing with his own ploy.

CHAPTER FOUR: **It's in the Cards**. One rummy player in the bunkhouse is humiliated by the others. The boy wonders how men can be so mean. He visits the mooring scow to watch poker and eat pastry made by Hardrock, the fascinating cook. The boy gets into trouble when he plays poker with the big boys.

CHAPTER FIVE: **The Gurry Pot Kid.** The boy nearly drowns when he falls into the watery slop in the cannery discharge pen, but entertains everyone else in the process. He begins to feel accepted in this adult male culture.

CHAPTER SIX: **Four Fisted Justice**. In a spontaneous strength contest a mild mannered mid-sized man carries 500 lbs. He and a partner clobber five or six attackers in a Ketchikan fight over a couple of "ladies".

CHAPTER SEVEN: **Ole, Ole'.** His morose trap partner thinks the boy is there to prevent illegal sale of their salmon. The boy narrowly avoids a probably lethal fight.

CHAPTER EIGHT: **Keep your Trap Shut.** A killer whale gets into a spiller full of fish. Frantic thrashing of this enormous creature threatens the fish, the spiller, the harvest season, and safety of the men. Miraculous timing brought a tender to the rescue.

CHAPTER NINE: **The Fortnight Legacy.** The boy reflects on his physical, personal and spiritual development.

CHAPTER TEN: **See Ya Next Year.** The boy says goodbye. Bigger, better, more mature, and richer, he sails for Seattle and his parents' welcome. What a summer it was!

CHAPTER ONE

Go North, Young Man

When we got to my dad's pride, a 1939 Plymouth, he asked me if I would like to drive us home. I grabbed the keys, dashed around the car, and climbed behind the wheel. I headed south along the Seattle waterfront, toward West Seattle. Suddenly, a west-bound car turned left in front of us. I yelled, "Watch out, you son-of-a-bitch."

After a long moment of silence, my mother said quietly, " Well, I guess he learned something up in Alaska."

That was the ending of my summer. What follows is the beginning.

Mom was her typical stoic self. Her tightened lips and stiffened body hid all but a few minor twitches in her quick embrace. But Dad, equally in character, nearly cracked my ribs with his wiry-armed hug. His eyes and mouth both lost composure, as he mumbled, "Goodbye, be careful".

I had none of their separation sadness. Instead, I

quivered with excitement tinged with apprehension. The slowly lifting morning fog hovered over us, as if forecasting the unknown changes awaiting me. I was embarking on a real adventure filled with physical demands, cultural changes and dangerous tasks. So my parent's misgivings were well founded.

This was June, 1939; and I, barely 17 years old, five feet, six inches tall, and weighing only 125 pounds, was going to work in the salmon fishing industry, with men much larger, stronger and decades older than I.

We were on pier 46, which reached into Elliot Bay, from the waterfront of Seattle, Washington. I was to board the U.S.S. Kodiak, one of the large Alaska Steamship Company vessels which carried passengers and freight to and from Seattle and Alaska. I was jauntily unprepared for a summer of working at a New England Fish Company cannery at remote Steamboat Bay, Noyes Island, Alaska. I knew little of what lay ahead, but could hardly wait to find out.

Harold E. 'Jack' Dempsey, our next door neighbor had offered me a job at this cannery, where he was assistant superintendent, bookkeeper and store manager.

"It'll be muscle building, physical work," he said. He knew I had just graduated from West Seattle High School, and was anxiously looking for work. "And you'll have a nice nest egg in a couple of months, if you work hard. You get transportation, board and room, 40 cents an hour, with lots of overtime pay. There's no place to spend money except at my little store, for a few clothes and personal stuff. But nothing else is needed, and there's no place to get it."

How's the food, Jack?" I asked.

Chuckling, he said, "More than even you can eat, and darned good, too. No fresh milk, though. No cows on the island. Only us guys, and a few natives. So if you can live without milk. and girls, and with a bunch of rough, tough men, you should end up with a full purse, and some stories to tell your grandchildren."

All this, plus travel and adventure on land and sea! What kid would have to think it over? Well, of course, my parents and their friends warned me of the dangers of salt-water fishing, but I assured them my duties would not include high risk activities. I really didn't know, but no self respecting seventeen year old boy would ever represent himself as anything but immortal.

The tide had gone out, allowing the exposed beach under the dock to emit pungent smells, and provide air space for the diving, shrieking seagulls to fight over the revealed tidbits. But I was oblivious to all but the call to board ship. With a quick last "Goodbye, I promise to be careful," I hoisted my duffle bag onto my shoulder, and scrambled across the gangplank.

As the steward showed me to my small stateroom I followed Jack's advice and gave him what was then a generous tip of $5.00. Jack said that this would assure me of good service for the two and one half day trip to Ketchikan. He was right. Steve not only looked after my things, but knowingly or not, helped with my latent social development.

In school I was seen as a nuisance, or as a "cute little kid with a mouthful of puns." My adolescent growth spurt started late, plus I was a couple of years younger than most of my classmates. In those days, if you were a quick learner you were moved ahead, regardless of your physical or social readiness. So I had some catching up to do in those areas. I was very envious of the other boys who were big enough to compete in high school sports.

When my envy led me to become a support manager for our football team, I talked a couple of the biggest guys into letting me scrimmage with them. Predictably, I broke my ankle. So much for extramural sports. But I did win the 95 lb. intramural wrestling trophy. I beat the only other kid who was that small.

Also, I was way behind socially. There was no 95 lb. class in dating . From at least age three I was strongly attracted to those wonderful creatures who were nicer, smelled better, and had such interesting contours. But even the smaller girls in high school liked more mature boys. Yes, I had a lot of catching up to do.

Our ship was about 300 feet long, with just enough staterooms on the upper deck for our 35-40 passengers. Only later did I discover that between the big cargo holds, fore and aft, were steerage quarters, occupied almost entirely by Asian men who worked in the canneries' fish processing lines. There was a nice dining room, also used for evening entertainment, and space for some deck games. But there was no swimming pool, casino, or ball-room. Spartan by today's cruise ship standards, it was seagoing magic to this excited, wide-eyed kid. I felt a tingle like my first carnival visit. This was better. It was real, lasting, and I was in the cast, not the audience.

There were two or three families on board, a number of professional men, and a few vacationing school teachers. No passengers were about my age, but I happily discovered that a nearby stateroom was occupied by two attractive young women of 19 or 20 years.

Evelyn was tall, with a well rounded and proportioned athletic build. She had shoulder length brown, almost auburn hair, and a slightly freckled, wonderfully friendly face. She was naturally warm, outgoing and inclusive, without being forward.

Jane was smaller, maybe five foot three inches tall, with a more lithe, but clearly feminine figure Her black hair was short; combed forward to frame a very pretty blue eyed face. Not really shy, rather she was more distant, alluringly confident, yet mysterious.

Since there was a dearth of eligible young men for them, and younger girls for me, we became shipboard friends, spending happy hours playing quoits, shuffleboard, and badminton, which I took to readily enough to win some of their praise. Jump for joy. It had worked. I had leaped over everything but the guard rail to impress them. Also, Steve helped by getting us seated together at meals. The two girls worked at clerical jobs in Tacoma, and had been friends for a long time. As they accepted me I became less self conscious. The girls in high school had treated me as a likeable, sometimes embarrassing kid brother. Now, there was little superficial patter, and I found it easy to reveal some of my worries and hopes, *e.g.* would I grow a few inches taller?

It was wonderful to feel liked and understood, but I had serious talks with myself about how to handle the sexual implications of my growing affection for them. "Which one do I like better? Probably Jane. She's prettier and more sexy, even though Evelyn does more for a sweater and is more friendly. Well, neither one has given me signals of personal encouragement, and I wouldn't know what the heck to do if they did. So just cool it, Jerry."

The first day passed quickly. Sunny weather spawned the deck games, and promoted frequent time-outs to view the astonishing scenery of the San Juan Islands, and their Canadian Gulf Island counterparts. Wildlife on shore, dolphins cavorting in the water, and the thousands of birds made us grateful for our slow, 12-15 knot pace. But even as daylight was extended by our northerly voyage another new experience awaited me that evening.

Steve, as ship's staff, was not allowed to fraternize with passengers. But he introduced us to the purser, Gilbert , whose officer status allowed more latitude. He quietly invited several of us, including Evelyn and Jane, to his stateroom after dinner. He served small glasses of port wine, cookies, and song recordings by Norman Lear. Wow! Tame by today's standards, the ribald lyrics reprised my guilty feelings when reading' Pep', or 'Spicy Detective', magazines, and hiding them under my mattress. I readily imagined it was I who was "having a time with Minnie the Mermaid, down in her seaweed bungalow:" Fortunately, none of the others noticed that I looked over my shoulder to see if my mother had sneaked aboard. Suave and cool, that was me.

The next morning, as I made my second brisk turn around the deck, Evelyn called, "Good morning, Jerry," from their open porthole.

I "helloed" back, and walked the few yards over to her. Just as I got close, she said, "Jane's still dressing".

Mumbling, "Oh, sorry", without much sincerity, I turned away, but not before glimpsing her beautiful bra and panty clad roommate.

Jane shrugged it off with a smile, and, "That's OK". I maintained gentlemanly stance, but mentally revisited that exciting image fairly often during the next few days.

The fair weather was holding, and the narrow straits of the inside passage brought us so close to shore it seemed like we could pick foliage from some of the over-hanging branches, or pet the nose of the fawn which stepped into the water toward us, as we passed by. Our usual salty air was filled with the sweet/sour smells of shore life, and spicy scents of new tips on the evergreens. My nose tickled, and my spirits soared.

As a farewell to the Ketchikan bound passengers there was an after dinner party. Each of us was intro-duced. I was acknowledged as the Mickey Rooney look-alike. He was well known in his Andy Hardy role, and I must have resembled him quite a lot, because I'd been stopped, even asked for autographs, by strangers, in Seattle. Unfortunately, neither Ann Rutherford nor Judy Garland was on board to co-star with me. Later, there was live music and dancing. As the balmy twilight faded, the moon, as well as early stars, softly illuminated the nearby deck.

Jane was dancing with some of the business men,

but Evelyn stayed in her deck chair, adjoining mine. Mostly our silence was broken by comments about the partying people. I wanted to ask her to dance , but lacked the courage. I felt I'd be embarrassed if she turned me down. Besides I lacked confidence as a dancer. Even though I had stage dancing experience in my pre-teen years, I was untrained in ballroom dancing. I had only recently convinced a classmate to attend the senior prom with me, and still hoped she didn't realize it was my first date.

So, while Evelyn and I sat close together, and shared some of our dreams, we didn't dance. I struggled with my warm feelings for her, tinged with incipient roman-tic ones, and wanted to put my arm around her. But, once more, I chickened out. Instead, I saw her to her room, thanked her for spending the evening with me, and went to my own room. I'll never know what her response might have been, if I'd been a little more bold. "Will I ever get off the dime?"

The next morning our ship made its way into the port of Ketchikan. Now my attention and excitement focused on what lay ahead. But at the top of the gangplank, Evelyn and Jane, who were continuing on to Juneau, gave me warm embraces. In a broken voice, I said, "I certain-ly wish I was older."

They were kind enough to say, " So do we."

Somewhat wiser, I put the missed opportunities behind me, lifted my heavy duffle bag, and headed down the pier to look for "Fearless" Dan Starkweather, skipper of the Cape Ulitka, bound for Noyes Island, and Steamboat Bay.

CHAPTER TWO

Puttin' on the Cape

I walked swiftly along the waterfront toward the floating piers, where the smaller boats were tied up. Soon, I spotted the Cape Ulitka, a wooden hulled boat, red, with white trim. My heart and pace quickened when I saw a man coming to meet me, arm waving.

It was, of course, Dan Starkweather, skipper of the Cape, as she was affectionately called. He gave me a big smile, a warm handshake, grabbed my duffel bag, and led me to the boat. "First trip north?" he asked. I nodded.

"Lots to see in town, but we need to shove off, in order to get to the cannery by tonight."

He was aboard smoothly, with two quick steps. He pointed behind him and said, "Gangplank is slippery."

Dan was about six feet tall, of athletic slender build, with almost shoulder length dark hair. Good looking, with brown eyes, friendly and unhurried.

I shook hands with the other members of the crew,

mate and engineer, Al North, and deckhand, Sidney Smallstone. In a few moments Al went below and started the engine. At Dan's bidding, I helped Sid bring in the lines, and we were underway. It was happening!

My hands trembled as I followed Sid's example in coiling the lines. Would I do things right? Would I fit in as I entered this work world of men, boats, sea and survival?

I had very little experience on the water. Other than a few fresh water fishing outings in rowboats, and a couple of ferry rides, I was a novice, a seagoing tenderfoot. Cruising a few feet above icy blue water made my nose tingle with its salty smell. I remembered Mom making me sniff salt water for a head cold.

My education began at once. Dan told Sid to "Show the kid around the boat." Sid grunted, " Uh huh."

He was obviously uninterested in my arrival. Slightly bigger and a couple of years older than I, he had streaky blond hair, and his clothes looked like they'd been pulled from the bottom of a full laundry chute. Although his vision was good, his pale blue eyes were like those of some blind people. He could look at you with no sign of recognition. I wondered if he didn't want anyone to get to know him.

In response to my questions, Sid told me the Cape was built around 1920, and served as a purse seine fishing boat until converted to a cannery tender a few years back. She was fifty four feet long, with a fourteen and a half foot beam, and draft of six feet when fully loaded. The hardwoods in the rails and gunwales showed their wear-burnished age, and the stained and slightly uneven decks smelled more of age than fish. She was clean, well maintained and shipshape.

Sid led me with, "C'mon," to the bow and the small forward hatch, then aft on the port side, past the pilot house, the head and the galley. Then we went to starboard, again past the pilot house, the captain's quarters, and to the ladders up to the flying bridge, and down to the crew's quarters. The main after deck, which was a couple of steps down, held a large winch, powered by the boat's engine. The winch controlled spooled steel cable to move a long boom carrying an oversized dip net. The net hoisted up to 300 salmon at a time into the hold of the boat, or into its scow alongside. Sid said as many as 6,000 fish, averaging five pounds each, could be loaded into the Cape. I said, "Oh, c'mon, Sid " in distrust of the hold's capacity. So Sid lifted up one of the hatch covers to show me the size of the hold. He laughed at me when I jumped back, holding my nose. Though scrubbed down hundreds of times, the oaken liner of that spacious hold still spewed out the remnant odors of its slimy marine occupants.

We then went below to crew's quarters, with bunks for four men. It smelled like a locker room with a bunch of yesterday's used towels. But pungent smell or not, I already hoped I'd get to throw my duffel bag on one of the bunks, as a member of the crew. What an adventure that would be.

Aft of these quarters was the engine room, and then

the bulkhead forming the forward wall of the hold. I was never very mechanically inclined, and knew absolutely nothing about marine engines, but I did notice the big metal wheel with holes in the rim. By this time I disliked Sid's limited and sullen responses, so I decided to wait and ask Al about the wheel.

Back topside, as we passed by the galley, the aroma of strong, freshly brewed coffee flavored the soft breeze. Dan called us to join him for a cup of joe. As I helped myself to a sweet roll, "provided by Harry, the cook at the cannery," he poured us coffee from a large blue-gray pot. This was no auto drip maker, nor even a percolator. The coffee was boiled, long and strong, sometimes with a raw egg in the basket with the grounds. Although I was not a coffee drinker at home I quickly formed a life long affiliation with that wonderful hot beverage, especially Alaska style with the added richness of sugar and canned milk.

We took our cups and one for Al, who was at the helm, to the pilot house, where I got my first lesson in steering the boat by reading compass points as well as directional degrees from north, *e.g.* NE is the same as 45 degrees.   Introducing me to dead reckoning, Dan showed me our present route, which was generally west, threading through small islands at the south end of the large Prince of Wales Island, which lies west of Ketchikan and extends over100 miles north. On our trip of about 110 nautical miles, we'd be within range of the native villages of Craig and Klawock, then on to the west coast of Prince of Wales Island, and head north to Noyes Island and Steamboat Bay. West of there is the vast, often stormy

Gulf of Alaska in the northeast part of the mighty Pacific Ocean.

I was involved hands-on right away. Dan showed me the next couple of course changes we would make, then had me use the straight edge to plot the lines on the chart while stating the readings by degree and by compass point Although nervous, I learned quickly. The math components of distances and times came easily, challenging and fun. But the biggest thrill came when Dan asked me if I'd like to take the helm.

When my shaking hands grabbed the wheel the boat began leaving herringbone stitches in the wake. Suffering through the laughter, and comments that my coffee must be laced with whiskey, I soon stopped over-steering, and stayed on course pretty well. Once again I was helped by the prior advice of my mentor, Jack Dempsey, who got me this job. He told me not to pretend I was smart.

"Admit you're ignorant, but anxious to learn. You'll be teased and tripped up anyway, but they'll be all over you if you pretend to know when you don't."

After this brief introduction to piloting, Dan asked Al to pick up where Sid had left off. "Now that he's seen the boat, maybe you can show Kelley what we do on it."

Al gave me a quick smile and said," Sure."

He added a wonderful balance to the gregarious

Dan Starkweather and the withdrawn Sidney Smallstone. Al was reserved, often quiet, yet always attentive and friendly. He had just finished his third year at the University of Washington, and had been at Noyes Island the two previous summers. Of average height, he looked husky. He had wavy brown hair and blue-green eyes complementing a slightly pug nose, which hinted of an Irish ancestor.

The sky began to cloud up, but rain held off, and we were shirt-sleeve comfortable out on the deck. I felt sort of overloaded with all the information Dan had fed me during the two hours or so I was in the pilot house. So the change was welcome. There was also lots to learn about deckhand work, but it was visible, tangible, and physical stuff, requiring less concentration. Much of it was how to handle the lines in various boat maneuvers, such as mooring, casting off or towing a scow. Al explained how a spring line was used to help bring the stern of the boat alongside a pier. He groaned in response to my facetious question, "No, a spring line isn't used only in April and May."

Years later I realized some of these basics I learned in Alaska were functionally better than what I was taught earlier in the Boy Scouts, or later in the U.S. Navy, or civilian boating classes. Among these fundamentals were: To first secure a line around the far prong of a cleat, rather than the near one; not to finish the figure eight wraps on a cleat with a half hitch; and be able to tie a bowline knot in the dark, and without first making a loop. These efficient and safer practices were probably handed down through generations of working men of the sea.

I asked Al about the wheel in the engine room.

He said, "That's called a flywheel, and it starts the engine. C'mon, I'll show you."

On the way below he explained that the engine was a 40 horse, 3 cylinder Atlas, started by manually turning the flywheel with a metal rod called a Johnson bar.

"This is stuck into one of the holes in the flywheel and cranked, much the same way as the old Model T Ford was cranked." Al added, "The engine's at least 20 years old, roughly the same vintage as the Model T. They don't make these anymore, but it's very reliable, and pushes us along at nine or ten knots."

Though the boat moved slowly, time sped by. How could I learn enough, fast enough? I was at sea in more ways than one. As I became aware of some of what I might be asked to do, I wondered, apprehensively, if I could handle my duties. But I could hardly wait for the chance.

As we went back topside Al asked me what I thought of this island scenery. I confessed that I was so immersed in absorbing all that I was being taught, that I paid scant attention to the small islands we passed by. I had noticed that some of them appeared undisturbed. Wildlife lived without competition from men. I hoped I'd get a chance to explore one of them sometime, but for now I was anxious to see the buildings and activities at Noyes Island.

As soon as we rounded the tip of Prince of Wales

Island we headed straight for, and into Steamboat Bay, arriving at dusk, which was about 11:00 p.m. We moved quietly to a floating pier, and tied up for the night. Dan told me I'd sleep on the Cape, but move into the bunkhouse in the morning.

I said, "Today was so great I was hoping I might get to stay on with you guys."

He patted my shoulder, replied," You did O.K. kid, maybe later on. In the meantime we'll see you in the mess hall, and hanging around the pier."

He pointed out the cannery building and two or three others, including the bunkhouse. Wow, I thought, "This is my home for the next six weeks. I'm ready."

Soon, we joined the rest of the cannery personnel in sleep preparation for the next day's work. As I laid my overstuffed head on my understuffed pillow I knew my heart was happy.

In spite of my excitement, the gentle rocking of the boat soon coaxed closure to my eyes.

CHAPTER THREE

The Noyes Makers.

I awoke easily at 6:00 a.m., when I heard the others stirring. Breakfast was to be at 7:00 and the workday to start at 8:00. As I went topside to the head I found the deck dampened by drizzle wrung from the passing gray clouds. Through the moist silence whispered the soft slurp of small debris rinsing itself against the pilings. A seagull scout squeakily complained that the cannery was not yet belching out its entrails. For now I was very happy with the briny sweet smell, which lingered in my breath.

The rest of the crew was up and ready to start the day. We climbed to the main deck of the cannery. It was actually a pier, about the size of two football fields, side by side. There was a large open space on the front, or sea end. All the loading and unloading was done there, and there was even a basketball hoop against the wall of the warehouse. We walked on two inch thick planks which were wear-polished to a weathered brown, especially in the front, where the thousands of cardboard cases of empty and then filled cans dropped from ship to shore, and back.

As we faced the shore there were two large buildings flanking the 18 foot walkway between them. The one on the left was the actual cannery, with all the mechanical equipment, and space for line workers seated at long conveyor belts. On the right was the warehouse with storage area serving as a workspace early on, and later as storage space for the cases of can bodies and lids soon to arrive. In the front of the warehouse was a small store, and offices for the two executives, Jay Bigelow, superintendent, and my mentor, Jack Dempsey, who was assistant superintendent, bookkeeper and store proprietor. The two men had an apartment above these quarters, and seldom fraternized with any of the workers.

As we got to the shore, the wide wooden walk divided and followed the shoreline in each direction. Straight ahead of us was a two-story dwelling, the bunkhouse, where machinists and other land based workers lived, and where I later found I was to go for a couple of weeks. But first, breakfast!

To the left a hundred feet or so, was the mess hall. It was a long narrow building which accommodated twenty five to thirty men seated on the two sides of the single table. The kitchen was at the far end of the building. We entered at the nearer, dining end. My nostrils and taste buds were already twitching at the smell of bacon and other morning treats. Now, as we entered, my telescoping eye could scarcely encompass the food on the table: cold cereal, oatmeal, ham, bacon, sausage, eggs fried or scrambled, toast, six inch sourdough pancakes, pastry, canned fruit and juice, and of course, pots of coffee.

It was a Sunday brunch on a Tuesday! I was a growing adolescent. An "appetite with hair" as one of them said. And breakfast was, and is, my favorite meal. Jack Dempsey needed do no more for me.

Unbelievably, this smorgasbord feast was repeated every morning. It was a consumption challenge, even for this growth spurt teenager. The two other meals, while of less variety, were as well prepared and generously served by Harry Nelson, the head cook, really a chef. For coffee breaks at 10:00 a.m. and 3:00 p.m. and for evening snacks, there were finger foods, leftovers, canned fruit and varieties of pastry. With six refills a day, my hungry stomach growls became mercy-seeking whimpers.

While we walked back to the Cape, I thanked Dan for showing me the boat and indicated I'd like to learn more, as a deckhand. He then revealed that I was to remain on shore for a while. He had me take my duffel bag with me as I went to meet Jack in his office. My dis-appointment at leaving the Cape did not dampen my enthusiasm, but I hoped I would get another chance at sea duty.

After we exchanged greetings, and I reported on our mutual neighbor families, Jack outlined what was ahead for me. I would be living in the bunkhouse with the men who stayed on shore and worked inside the cannery, or on the grounds. I would start by helping the crew working on the warehouse floor behind his office. They were piecing together the wire fence to be suspended from the fish trap logs. He explained that the salmon fishing season dates varied according to the method of catching them. The first open dates were later that week and included taking fish by trolling, done on small sea-going boats, outfitted with four long poles, each holding a single line to hook one fish at a time. These were customarily one-man boats.

Many more fish were taken by purse seiners. These ranged from about the size of the Cape, which was a seine boat originally, to boats up to 90 feet in length. They circled schools of fish with a net which, while floating at the top, could be closed, or pursed, at the bottom, then gradually tightened until the fish could be dipped out, a process known as brailing.

"So the cannery will start operating as soon as the fish arrive," Jack said. "But in the meantime we have to get traps ready for their short season, which begins in two weeks. The traps are the source of 70 - 75% of our production."

Jack also advised that I would have to join the Alaska Fishermen's Union, a branch of the West Coast Longshoremen's Union, headed by the controversial Harry Bridges. I had no objection. "However," Jack went on, "You're supposed to be at least 18 years old."

There seemed to be no choice, except lying, but I was very uncomfortable about doing so. Later, when we met with Jan Starvik, the union representative, he eyed me suspiciously and asked if I was really 18.

I said, "Yes."

"What year were you born in?"

Slight pause, "1921."

"Could I see your driver's license?"

"I knew there were no cars here so I left it at home."
Another lie. I saw myself on my way back to Seattle.

Jan looked to Jack, who shrugged slightly and said,
"I know he just graduated from high school."

Finally Jan said, "Well, OK, but you'd damn well better do the work of an 18 year old."

As if I needed more incentive.

As we left the office, heading for the bunkhouse we
saw the back of a large, white haired man with, what I
found out later, was a 150 pound bag of coal on his shoulder. As we watched him climb the long front steps, Jack
told me this was "Hans, a Dutchman who used to be first
mate on the tall ships, and was now the custodian - well,
really the boss, of the bunkhouse".

Up close, Hans was really impressive - 6 ft 3 or 4,
about 220 pounds of lean strength. I found it hard to
believe I was seeing the face of a man 80 years old, give
or take a couple. What a force he must have been as a
ship's officer!

As we shook hands his weathered face was impas-

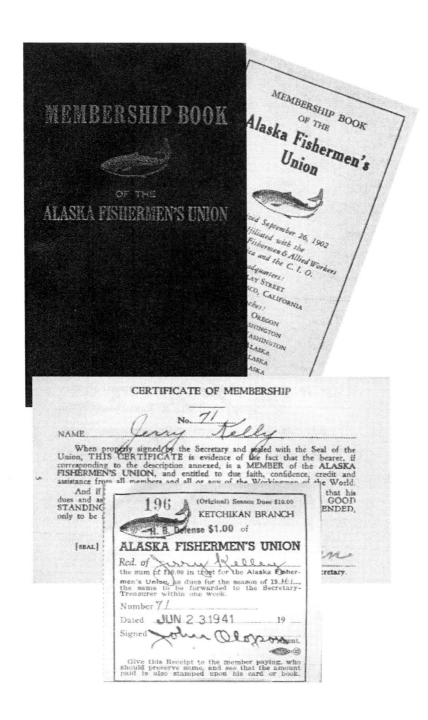

sive, but he was kind enough to leave my hand uninjured. He turned out to be mostly a loner, taciturn, but he always made sure that the place was clean and orderly, including us. No wonder. His very presence would quell escalating arguments.

Soon I joined the four or five man work force in the warehouse. We were preparing equipment for the fish traps. The basic trap structure was a series of large logs attached together, and anchored 1,000 feet off shore. A one inch steel cable was secured on shore and stretched out to the trap. The cable was floated by being stapled to wooden railroad ties every couple of feet. Then the chicken wire fence was suspended from the cable, shore to trap, and unfolded to lengths matching the depth of the water. This was named the "lead". It led the fish into the trap.

When in place, this wire barrier confronted the salmon, swimming along the shore in preparation for entering a river to spawn. The fish were then forced to follow the lead, away from shore, through several tunnels, decreasing in size, and ultimately into the large net pens, called spillers, from which they were brailed into the cannery tenders, or fish scows they were towing.

In the warehouse six-foot wide rolls of chicken wire were uncoiled, a bit at a time, and laid out on the floor. At preplanned intervals the wire was cut into lengths. These layers were then added in stair step fashion, forming a hanging barrier about 600 ft long and from 5 to 50 ft in depth. Each section followed closely the actual changes in depth of the water for each trap.

To assemble the layers we used pliers with jaws, called hog ringers, which were channeled on the inside to hold ¾" wide steel hog rings, that closed as connectors. It took about all the hand power I had to bend the ring ends together. By the time I finished work that first day my right hand was beginning to swell, as well as hurt. Not so bad, however, that I was unable to negotiate my way through another of Harry's meals.

After supper we went back to the bunkhouse. By this time I had met most of the other residents. As Jack had instructed, I did not try to impress them. Rather, I was respectful, let them lead, and assessed this new bunch of men. Theirs was more brain and skill work than the physical demands of the guys who worked on the boats and scows. Once again, I was excited by the new challenges. I was a little anxious, but innocently optimistic.

One of the most interesting fellows was a tall, slender machinist with mischievous eyes and facile wit and speech. His name was Ernie G. Miner. I was quite a curiosity to this group of seasoned dormitory dwellers. The youngest of them was in his late thirties. They began to make kidding and friendly references to having a nice young boy around, especially since there were no girls to help pass the time.

Ernie was enjoying the banter. Then he interjected, with a slightly wicked tone, "Say lad, I have a strong interest in ornithology. How'd you like to go bird watching with

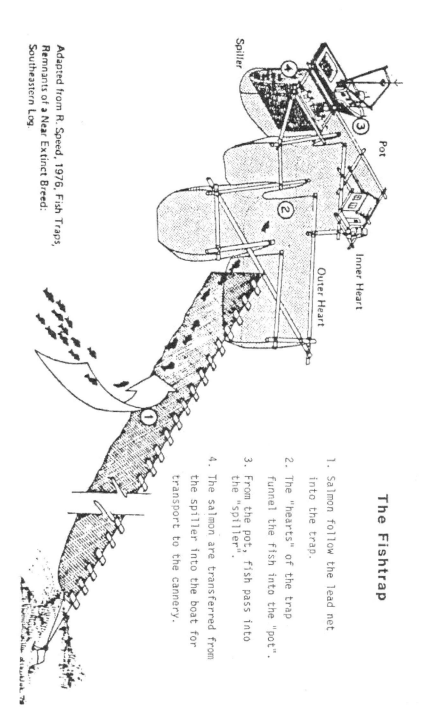

Spiller

Pot

Inner Heart

Outer Heart

Adapted from R. Speed, 1976, Fish Traps,
Remnants of a Near Extinct Breed:
Southeastern Log.

The Fishtrap

1. Salmon follow the lead net
   into the trap.

2. The "hearts" of the trap
   funnel the fish into the "pot".

3. From the pot, fish pass into
   the "spiller".

4. The salmon are transferred from
   the spiller into the boat for
   transport to the cannery.

me? I could teach you about the sea birds of Noyes Island." The rest of the guys snickered.

Although I was very naïve about some sex stuff, I figured out what was going on, but sensed the implication was teasing, not propositional and quickly decided to play along.

"Sure," I said. "You can introduce me to all your gull friends."

To a chorus of catcalls we were off. Ernie held the door for me, and made some gesture, which caused more hooting.

The walk was enjoyable. We began to get acquainted, and he really did know quite a bit about birds. He pointed out several varieties of gulls, and he told me the joke about leaving no tern unstoned.

When we got back to the bunkhouse Ernie opened the door and said, "After you."

"Oh, no," I said. "I learned my lesson. You go first this time."

The applause and raucous laughter told me I had passed my first test.

CHAPTER FOUR

It's in the Cards`

Recreation and social life at the cannery were limited. If it wasn't raining some of the men would hang around the pier, smoking and swapping yarns and fables. But rain or shine the main gathering place was the large living room in the bunkhouse. It served as a lobby entrance to the bedrooms on the first floor and the stairs to the second. Mainly, it extended a warm welcome as a place to congregate when the work of the day was done.

As I entered, on the left stood a round table big enough for eight card players at the nightly rummy games, while across on the right side were three square tables for up to four men each, mostly competing at checkers or cribbage. There were rocking chairs, and floor lamps supplementing the room lights. But the dominant fixture was a fifteen inch green shaded gambling hall light overhanging the round table. Halfway down the left side was the tall coal burning stove which Hans, the resident caretaker, never allowed to die out. Despite his efforts, a little of the coal smoke escaped when the fire was at ember stage. That acrid smelling smoke clung to the rising heat, and spiced the edges of the tobacco smoked ceiling.

Almost everyone used tobacco. Some smoked store bought cigarettes, some carried little cloth bags of Bull Durham tobacco flakes and packets of papers to roll them in. My new friend Ernie showed off by rolling his cigarette with one hand, licking the paper with a flourish. A few added a fireplace-like odor to the gathering haze with their pipes. Occasionally cheap cigar smoke curled into the mix. Then there were the chewers. Some fat cigars were not lighted, but gradually chewed away. Other guys used plug cut tobacco, or the fine cut snuff, often called 'snoose'. The resultant juices were spat into the several polished brass spittoons, their arced landings pinging against the metal.

There were no ping pong, billiard, or other gaming tables. And no alcohol. Every evening there were players and spectators around the card tables. At the small tables, cribbage was usually played just for fun. But the six or seven regulars at the round table played very serious two deck rummy, at twenty five cents a game.

I knew I was a fresh curiosity, but this card playing culture made it a lot easier for me to fit in. During my childhood years of the 1920s, and especially the 30s, when money was so scarce, families relied heavily upon themselves for recreation. Early on I had spent many happy hours playing hearts, rummy, pinochle and poker. Also, I had always enjoyed and been good at numbers games. Hence, in a short time I became one of the better cribbage players. Much earlier I had learned not to let my competitiveness and rather short fuse result in discourteous behavior at cards. So I now thanked my opponents/teachers, praised others for good play, and attributed my success to good luck.

As I was gaining trust I began to kibitz the rummy games. As long as I kept my mouth closed, a feat the others thought somewhat remarkable, I was allowed to move slowly around the table, studying the players or their cards. Spying was easy except for Burt Proctorville, one of the several machinists.

He was a large man who moved slowly, his evenly distributed weight drawing muffled groans of protest from the flooring. Burt appeared to be about fifty years old with proportionally large head and face. His deep set eyes were standing guard like gunnery pill boxes in a hillside. They were not furtive, but brooding and suspicious.

Burt watched intently for any sleight of hand or other sign of possible unfair play. Even when they injected humor or other banter into the game, Burt seemed more solemn and withdrawn over these deviations from regular play.

Each player had room enough to hide his holding from the eyes of the others. However, it was easy for us watchers to see the cards from behind. Not so with Burt. His huge fleshy hands cupped around the cards, occasionally revealing one of them momentarily, like a shy exhibitionist. Except when he played his cards only he could see the identifying edges. All I ever learned from peering into his domed hand was how best to hide my own in later games.

Of course, he was easy psychological prey for the likes of Ernie and his buddies. When Burt confessed that he thought cats were bad luck, and that he hated the untamed ones which lived around the cannery, a plot was hatched. They found some greenish-brown heavy grease, molded it into fecal shaped curls, and placed it, along with cat paw prints, on Burt's desk in the cannery. Burt's near-hysterical anger at "the God damn cat" brought on laughter and heavy teasing. When he realized he was the victim of a prank, his face, flushed with anger, blanched with embarrassed frustration. His bulky body heaved as he fought to control rage and hurt. Then, wrapped in dark gloom, he trudged off to his room to be alone with his humiliation. Burt was absent from the evening games for about a week. Judging from the subdued character of the place, I think everyone regretted the whole practical joke, but I doubt Burt ever received much sympathy, let alone apology.

Probably I didn't even know the word paranoia then. But I learned that not all of us are able, emotionally, to handle all the competitive ragging so characteristic of men in groups. And why did heckling sometimes seem harmless? I was being picked on frequently for my ignorance, my youth, my appetite and my smart- ass remarks. But I took it as part of my learning and there was always a light-hearted quality to it. Why was someone like Burt so vulnerable, and why were the others so cruel?

The lively atmosphere of the bunkhouse was never the same after that incident, but my transient status helped protect me from the somber quietness.

Anyhow, I kept hearing about another social center at Steamboat Bay that sounded well worth investigation. So I set out to see what was afloat.

The largest vessel moored at the cannery was not a boat. It was a barge, about 30 by 75 feet, with some housing at the stern, which provided sleeping quarters for a small crew, a galley, and dining area. Mid-ship was a big steam engine, a huge winch, and heavy duty stanchions, cleats and other equipment that defined this barge as a rigging scow, sometimes called a mooring scow. The forward open deck provided work space and room for temporary cargo.

This was the work center for nearly all of the cannery facilities located away from Steamboat Bay. Most of the salmon were caught in large traps anchored off shore, and the rigging scow was critical to setting the traps in place. Some such scows were self propelled, but ours was towed to location by our largest cannery tender, the A .F. Rich.

Thick timbers made up the body and floor of the scow. Even the galley floor was pock marked from the caulks of "corked boots", as they were called. Little metal spikes protruded from the soles, like those of track or golf shoes. They were necessary for walking on the flattened trap logs, and to avoid slipping on the scow floor in wet windy weather. The place was clean, but worn and seasoned, with shallow stained ruts that formed pod cultures, mixing smells of fish and old machine oil, as they climbed the heavy salt air. However, setting out the traps was yet to come. My interest in the rigging scow was far less complex and impersonal. I had found out that the more adventuresome guys spent evenings playing poker on the scow. I wanted to assess these games as I had the rummy games in the bunk house. Furthermore, though I had no complaint about Harry's "coffee break" offerings, there were rumors of tasty pastry, including my favorite, crullers, from the creative hands of Hardrock, the cook on the scow. My moist taste buds remembered many dawn excursions back home.

For the past year or so I ended my early morning Seattle Post Intelligencer paper delivery at the bakery on the corner of Fauntleroy and California Avenues in West Seattle. For one thin dime I got a bag full of day-old butterhorns, maple bars, and crullers. I shared them with my mixed breed dog, Rusty, as we walked home. Then, while digesting the pastry, we both caught an hour's sleep before Mom called us to breakfast. The high carb and sugar intake prepared me well for the pastry of Harry and Hardrock. Rusty survived well, too. He died six years later at age twenty-one. The next night, looking for cards and crullers, I made my way down to the dock. The two or three guys from the bunk house grunted, "Hello" as they looked up from the poker table. The other players, who were housed in the scow or tenders, only nodded. I waited until that hand was over before moving toward the galley, looking for the snack counter. At that, one of the players said, loudly, "You must be the new kitchen dweller I've heard about. Help yourself." The voice, of course, belonged to Hardrock.

The rumors about his pastry were right. Later, when I found out he had acquired his nickname because of the density of his first biscuits, I struggled to reconcile that story with his skill with dough --- both kinds, as it turned out. He was also the most consistent winner at the quarter ante and five dollar limit poker games, and easily the most fascinating of all the men on Noyes Island.

Most of the scow and tender crews were lean, muscular, very tough men who worked as loggers in the winter and for the cannery during summers, when fire hazards often resulted in closing down tree harvesting. Many came from Scandinavian stock and were the epitome of the rugged blue collar men who formed the backbone of our country's tangible physical growth. They ranged in age from early 30s to mid 50s.

Hardrock was cut from different fabric. He had the more well groomed and cleaner appearance one expects of a cook. He was in his mid forties, about five foot eleven inches tall, with a trim build. His dark blond hair, beginning to thin, showed a few strands of gray. It was a little shaggier than his well trimmed sideburns. There were no barbers nearby to finish his rather suave look. His green/gray eyes danced with both merriment and wary control. His neat, medium sized moustache seemed to punctuate his facile speech.

He had worked and traveled widely on the sophisticated fringes of legitimacy. His tales of being a bellhop, carnival sideshow barker, con man and lover, were mesmerizing. A master raconteur, he was also spontaneously wicked. He knew he was in charge of all non-cannery discussions. He was smooth. Even this brief exposure to Hardrock was captivating. I had never met anyone like him. I thought such men existed only in movies or books, and probably I was not supposed to know about them. I fell asleep wondering if I would ever have such exciting, if questionable, adventures.

On the following evening, in my efforts to appear mature and worldly, I showed up smoking a pipe filled with aromatic tobacco flavored with maple sugar. Hardrock grimaced, waved the smoke away, and groaned, "My God, Kelley, I haven't smelled anything that bad since I was last in a Panamanian whorehouse." Once more I was an easy mark for entertainment. The several others who regularly smoked pipes filled them with Granger rough-cut tobacco, which I thought should have been "rough throat." My throat felt raw for three days when I tried some. Anyhow the guys loved retelling my encounter with Hardrock, and my sissy tobacco.

A few nights later, as I headed for the treats, Hardrock called out, his now familiar greeting, "Well, here comes my pet seagull." This time I stopped and asked, "Why do you call me your pet seagull?" "Like them, all you do is eat, shit and squawk." Amid the chorus of laughter I went into the galley, grabbed two or three crullers, went back to the game, and announced, "Here's the first part, eating. For the next phase you'll need to come back tomorrow morning." There were a few chuckles as some of them kept up with me. Hardrock laughed heartily, then asked if I wanted to take the place of an absent poker player. I had been wondering what I would do if such a chance came. I had played poker quite a few times with family and buddies at home, often enough for me to learn to conceal my nervousness and animation. But we had played for matchsticks, or at most, pennies. Could I keep my cool with these serious players for much higher stakes? I had been kibitz-studying them and their play for several nights. Maybe I could transfer my amateur poker face into their game. So, with all the nonchalance I could muster, I said, "Hey you guys have to take it easy on me," and sat down.

After a cautious beginning, my cards improved and I began to win fairly often. Most of the bets were twenty-five cents, so the pots were only two to three dollars. Still, after about an hour I was up about fourteen dollars, and some of the others were beginning to grumble about beginner's luck. The tension made me even more nervous, so I played extra conservatively, but I still did well. The cards were with me. On the last hand, a five card stud game, my first two face up cards were Jacks. I was high, but only bet a quarter. I called a couple of raises which appeared based on flush or straight possibilities. My next card up was a seven. I checked, but called the several bets of others. With the final cards, two players paired up with aces or kings, respectively. My card was a third Jack and I bet three dollars. After much thought each of the others folded. No one had hit what he hoped for, nor had the courage to bluff. Too bad. I was lying in wait. They never knew that my hole card was the fourth Jack.

  With the last big pot my winnings were thirty- seven dollars, a small fortune in my life. Gosh, I thought, I made half a month's wages in a couple of hours! I hid my shaking hands in my pockets as Hardrock said, "I wonder if my pet seagull has turned into a shark?" He was half joking, but the muttering of the others about "getting even" was not friendly. Still trembling from the excitement of winning, I felt my stomach knot at the hostility. I wanted to turn and run, but, acting unconcerned, eased my way up to the dock. I was long awake. The log I usually slept like was tossed by waves of anxiety that night.

CHAPTER FIVE

The Gurry Pot Kid

Word travels fast. At breakfast the news of my winnings winged around the table like a mosquito in a nudist colony. When it reached Sidney, the unfriendly dull deckhand on the Cape, he jabbed me with a loud, "Well Kelley, you finally found something you're good at." It was probably his wittiest remark ever. I resisted the urge to reply caustically, because everyone was listening, so I replied, "No, Sid, I'm still looking. That was just damn good luck." I fielded other comments pretty much the same way that morning, but dreaded my inevitable meeting with Jack Dempsey. Sure enough, at noon he pulled me aside. After confirming that "Yes, I had played poker with the big boys," he virtually forbade me from such games. His lecture was short, but brutally clear. He felt they would be out to get even, and more, and I was far too innocent to cope with such experienced and formidable men.

Of course I followed his advice, since my very presence there was dependent upon his avuncular care. The other players gradually softened and discarded their resentment over not having the opportunity to recoup their losses. Hardrock rose above the revenge motive, and actually served as a buffer for his "pet seagull" who continued to devour his pastries.

Previously, I was a frequent object of curiosity and amusement to the rest of the men. I was innocent, gullible, full of adolescent energy and blissfully unaware of being so newsworthy. Now, after the poker game, I felt like an annoyance, even a disturbance to some of the men. They, as well as I, wondered what would be next.

The arrival of the first big freighter to unload the many boxes of can lids and bodies brought my first opportunity to be a longshoreman. Pallets full of these cardboard cases were lowered from the ship to the dock, and then into the warehouse by forklift. Several of us then carried the boxes from the pallets and stacked them up for later use.

The boss of this crew was Jan Starvik, the union rep who had warned me to "do the work of an eighteen year old," because he was skeptical of my actual age. I was trying to impress him, and the other men as well, so I all but ran while carrying the forty pound boxes . "I'll show them," I said to myself as I passed them by. Well, in almost no time I noticed the guys were not talking much. There was a natural rhythm, like a choreographed march, to the box carrying procession, and I was out of step. Jan stopped me.

"Kid, we're being paid by the hour, not by each unit, like piecework. We've got several hours of work yet, so we all need to keep an even pace. This ain't a race."

"Gosh, you told me to do a man's work."

"Yeah, but I didn't have Jesse Owens in mind. Just watch me. Nice and steady. Remember we're getting time and a half pay. We want to earn it honestly, but without short changing ourselves."

Everybody relaxed, and later on I was very grateful for the slower pace. I was exhausted, while the others appeared as strong as ever. No wonder Jesse never ran any race longer than the 220.

Each day brought new challenges. I still had a lot to learn about the work, the men, and the whole operation which burst into new sounds, smells and activities a couple of days later when the first fish arrived and the canning began.

At the outboard side of the cannery was a metal chute through which all the fish residue discharged. Much of the gutting and cutting of the salmon, and filling of the cans, was done by a machine called the "Iron Chink," a term I disliked, but didn't realize why until a few years later, when I became conscious of the evils of race prejudice and stereotyping. In fact many Chinese immigrants were displaced by these machines. All of the heads, tails, entrails and discarded parts of the salmon dropped into a floating chicken wire pen called the gurry pot. It was, indeed, pot shaped, about eight feet deep, and eighteen feet square. At the end under the discharge chute, the wire formed a trap door, like the drop seat of long johns. The whole wire pot hung from a framework of flattened logs. There was also a three by twelve inch plank nailed across the middle of the log square.

Once the canning started, and all the leftovers spilled into the gurry pot, my senses quickly told me about it. The seaward breeze carried both the fetid smell, and the primitive cries of warring gulls fighting for sea and air supremacy. I had little desire to become more intimately acquainted with this battle zone, but as the employee with the least seniority, I was told to put on my new hip boots and report to the captain of our largest tender, which was stern-tied to the gurry pot. The boat was the A. F. Rich, and the skipper, Carl Danielson, was a man in his early thirties, friendly, but very task oriented and disciplined.

He said, "You've probably wondered what we do with this smelly mess when it gets full every few days, like it is now. Well, we untie the pot, tow it out to the mouth of Steamboat Bay, open up the apron at the drop end, and flush out the whole thing. And you, Kelley, have the privilege of riding on the plank so you can loosen the lines and make it all happen." Carl gave me a few more specific instructions, and asked if I was ready.

"Yes sir, it sounds like fun except for the smell." Actually, this close it was so pungent, my eyes began to water.

"Be careful," he added.

"Don't worry. I walked on wet fallen logs lots of times in Schmitz Park when I was a kid…. well, a younger kid."

I was also accustomed to this drizzly weather, so typical of Seattle as well as here, so I was full of confidence when I walked out on the framework logs, and untied the pot mooring lines. I waved up to Carl on the flying bridge of the Rich, and started out on the plank over the teeming slurry, to select a nice view-level seat for my ride. When I took my third jaunty step I did a half gainer into the putrid marine morass. Fortunately, I hit feet first, so my head was clear of the water. I sank slowly because the slimy mixture was so thick, but as my hip boots began to fill I was barely able to crawl/swim the two feet or so to reach the plank again. I pulled myself sideways to the nearest log, where helping hands braved the smell and my slippery body, to yank me out.

I vaguely realized that there was a lot of yelling and swearing by Carl and his crew when I fell in. But I was too busy surviving to pay much heed at the time. So my vocabulary remained un-enhanced. However, memory of a similar brush with death came flooding back. My family was picnicking at Lake Sammamish, east of Seattle.

I was about twelve, and rowed a small boat out to an old abandoned pier, to see if I could outwit some of the fish that often hang around the pilings of such structures. Turned out there was a bunch of loose logs, cordoned off between me and the pier. I found a log with a handy nail to tie the boat. Then I picked up my rod, tackle box, can of worms, and jar of salmon eggs, and started to skip across the dozen or so of the floating logs. The eighth or ninth log rolled at my step. I was incredibly lucky. Like a Halloween apple I bobbed up between the logs. Had I come up under a couple of the two foot wide logs, divers might have been the ones to find me. Well, with a few kicks and log-supported elbows I nudged over to the pier, and clambered up. Once safe, my inventory revealed only the eggs were missing. But the fish preferred the worms anyway. After a couple of hours I had caught some fish, dried off in the sun, and figured out what I was going to tell my parents. It was only then that I realized how narrowly I had survived my stupidity, and began to shake.

After a few minutes I calmed down enough to pick up my gear, and the eleven fat perch I had caught, and walked the shoreline back to the picnic area. I told my folks I couldn't get back to the boat because the logs had drifted away from the pier. I'm not sure they believed me, but probably let it drop as long as I was okay. We took another boat out to retrieve the first one.

That flashback added old fear to the new awareness of escaped danger. Once more I began to shake. I think cold water shivering hid my fright from the others. Simultaneously, I was greeted with a chorus of laughter, shouts and applause. A crowd had gathered as though free show tickets had just been handed out. Someone had spread the word that the guileless lad was embarking on another adventure.

My gurry pot cruise had to be delayed long enough for me to be hosed off, which, of course, elicited more raucous glee from the spectators. Then I had to change clothes. There was no way to get the stench out of my new boots, so they were later burned in a ceremonial pyre. Much too late, I realized that the logs in Schmitz Park were not glazed with bird poop and fish slime as were these. Talk about learning the hard way! Through this whole affair I tried to hold my head up, and join the others in laughter at my misfortune, but I wanted to sneak away and cry. I wasn't as devastated as Burt had been when ridiculed, but I was greatly embarrassed, and worried that I was being seen as a buffoon, rather than a likeable useful apprentice. I figured my best chance at honest but supportive counsel was with Hardrock.

I found him relaxed between lunch cleanup and dinner preparation. He already knew what had happened and was about to razz me until he saw my serious face. I told him I didn't know how to handle this. "What do you do if you've really made an ass of yourself? " He paused, lighted a cigarette with a match stick, exhaled the long first drag of smoke, then looked at me with a warm half-smile. "Well, let me tell you how I got my nickname of Hardrock. I was working for a carnival that went belly-up in Hoquiam, Washington. A friend told me the cook of a nearby logging camp had just been let go. Well, hell, those loggers were not exactly connoisseurs of fine food. So I figured I could bluff my way through. I guess they were desperate, 'cause I got the job, and the next day they were throwing my first biscuits to the crows. But they were glad to have a cook who could speak more than a few words of English."

"The one before you was a foreigner?" I asked. "Yeah, a Chinese immigrant. The guys said they'd been teasin' the hell out of him, you know, about pigtails, slant eyes, yellow skin and shuffle feet. Apparently, he was as inscrutable as folklore says. He never said a word about being picked on. Just cooked and served. Finally, they got so guilty they called him in , told him they were sorry, and wouldn't tease him anymore.

When they finished apologizing the Chinese cook said; 'Hokay, me no more pissee in soup.'

They fired him and got me, with my dense biscuits. They hung in there with me, and I got to be a pretty good cook. So…better give these guys, and yourself another chance." He was a sage, and a forecaster. I swallowed my pride, and soon realized that most of them, with the exception of Sidney, seemed glad, not glum or indifferent, when I showed up. But for the rest of the summer I often heard, "Hey, here comes the gurry pot kid!"

CHAPTER SIX

Four Fisted Justice

It was a rare Noyes Island afternoon, actually sunny. Simmered steam rose from drizzle puddles heated by the sun. Soggy gray skies turned cloudless blue. For a moment the warmth took me back to Alki Beach in Seattle, and my sneaked glimpses of feminine parts yet un-tanned. But the sun also released an energy surge which pushed aside the tempting fantasy. The weather change lifted all our spirits. Work pace quickened, chatter was livelier and mood happier. My natural sense of optimism was buoyed by the warmth and my growing confidence as a member of this productive crew. We were lowering the last of the layered chicken wire bales, and other supplies, from the pier to the mooring scow. These and other heavy and bulky items were lifted by the long boom on the scow, then secured on the deck to protect against movement during heavy seas. There was special excitement in the summer air. The last of our four traps was to be anchored in place the next day, and opened for business the following Saturday. The traps would be teeming with hundreds, even thousands of salmon, unaware they were assembling to be harvested by us.

As we finished with the bales of wire, the crew boss, Jan Starrvik told me to help the men on the scow. "But first," he said, "see if the guys on the Oregonian need a hand." The Oregonian was the mid-sized boat of our three cannery tenders. It stretched out at seventy- four feet. Although built as a purse seiner it had a leaner look and was handsomely attired in a newly painted red coat trimmed with white. The boat had made a trip to Ketchikan for kitchen/galley supplies. A couple of men I had not met were starting to unload huge bags of flour, carrying them up the ramp, at about a fifteen degree angle.

I grunted and caught my breath as I picked up a bag, and followed the guy ahead who saw me struggle with the weight. In a strong Scandinavian accent he sneered, "Maybe you should grow up some more before you try to carry one hundred twenty-five pounds." This brooding man turned out to be Ole Hemmigstead, whom I would later get to know all too well when we spent a couple of weeks together in close quarters. For now I didn't respond to his snide remark. While gasping for breath it was all I could do to labor up the gangplank and drop the bag onto the forklift trailer. As I turned, I gasped again. The man behind me had one bag over his left shoulder and another tucked under his right arm. He easily climbed the ramp, and winked as he passed this open-mouthed kid. I confirmed later that the bags did weigh one hundred twenty-five pounds each.

This muscular, ruddy complexioned man looked as Irish as his name, Donegal Casey. His face was somewhat square, with smile wrinkles under the eyes.

Features were nice and even, except for the slightly wide nose, which was mauled a little to the left. His long red locks and flashing green eyes evoked images of Celtic warriors I had read about. With his looks and athletic strength he seemed larger than his actual five foot eleven inch and one hundred eighty- five pound physique.

As I recalled Jack Dempsey's admonition to never cross any of these men, I said to myself, "Amen." I had never before seen arm and shoulder muscles that rippled even while at rest. More such power display was to come.

I struggled up to the dock two or three more times, hollered, "Gotta go help on the scow," and started off. Donegal quickly overtook me, patted me on the shoulder and said, "You did OK, kld." I glowed.

I joined the group of five or six who were working with the trap equipment. Everything had to be placed in a compact area on the deck of the scow, ready to be unloaded later. Included were the 1,000 ft spool of steel cable, which would be the umbilical cord sustaining the trap from the shore; the railroad ties to keep the cable afloat; the kegs of four inch staples to hold the cable on the ties; and the bales of layered chicken wire to hang from the cable to the sea bottom, forming a fenced high-way for the fish to follow into the trap spillers.

These were two net pens, called spillers, because from them the fish were spilled into the boats or scows. About twenty feet square and ten feet deep, these nets were suspended from floating logs. In order to maintain an open box shape, the bottom corners of the netting were held down by cast iron weights. These were hexangular, ten inches wide, fifteen inches tall, with a large upside down U-bolt handle at the top. They each weighed two hundred and fifty pounds.

As the men were dragging or edge rolling the weights into place, one of them bent his knees, grabbed the handle with both hands, lifted the weight, and swung it forward a few inches. Immediately, there was a contest. Another guy moved his weight a couple of feet. When they saw my dropped jaw and bugged out eyes I was invited to give it a try. Well, that's exactly what it was, a try. Even though I was gaining strength every day, from the hard physical work, I failed to do more than tilt the weight and pull it a few inches. My disappointment and chagrin were offset by good natured cheers of, "Nice going, Kelley." Despite my dashed hopes I really felt a sense of inclusion.

The next competitor was "Hugo, the Hammerer" so called because of his legendary prowess with the top maul, a sledge hammer he used to staple the cables onto the ties keeping the cables afloat. Hugo was the largest of the men. In his mid-forties, he stood about six foot two and weighed around one hundred and ninety pounds, with long sinewy arms and big hands. He stood out, what with his size, and a handsome face with dark bushy mustache caressing the corners of his mouth. In contrast, he was a very quiet, rather withdrawn man who had to be urged to participate. His height was a disadvantage, since he had farther to crouch and farther to lift. However, he had no trouble lifting the weight, and carrying it about seven or eight feet, to considerable clapping and cheers. The two hundred fifty pound weight carried between the legs caused a duck-like walk, which evoked some humorous chuckles.

Then Donegal stepped up. Since most of the others were of Scandinavian stock, he probably had ethnic pride motivating him, along with his natural extravertish person-ality. Having seen how he handled the flour bags, I had no doubt he would excel. He crouched, took a couple of deep breaths, picked up the weight, and wobble-walked it the full fifteen feet. With great flair he lifted it up onto a sling board about a foot above the floor. With a little bow, he turned and strolled back to the group. The others were good sports, and included praises with a few jeers of "show off."

There were two weights left. Donegal put his arm on the shoulder of the man next to him. "Your turn, Clarence," he said. This was a pleasant, soft spoken, rather reserved man of probably thirty-seven years. He was neither Scandinavian nor Irish, but a French/Canadian named Clarence Germaine. I knew him a little from my frequent visits to the poker games and Hardrock's pastry table. He was of average size and appearance, with dark hair. His eyes were often serious and intense. He was no taller than five foot ten and weighed about one hundred seventy-five pounds. His build was not obviously muscular, like Donegal's, but he moved with the natural grace of a gifted athlete, or mascu-line dancer like Gene Kelly. Because of his last name. Germaine, he was sometimes referred to as "Geranium, the flower of Noyes Island." But no one called him that to his face. Soon, I found out why.

Clarence went over to the remaining trap weights, spit on his hands, bent his knees, and straightened up with one weight in each hand. Then, he walked slowly the whole distance, and gently lowered the weights to the floor.

There were gasps and muffled invocations. The feat was too impressive for applause.

Clarence shook his arms to loosen them up, stretched for a moment, then quietly rejoined Donegal who greeted him with a huge smile and a hug.

Shortly after, I collared my buddy Hardrock who had watched all this, to express my awe at the strength of these men, especially Donegal and Clarence. He said they were functionally far more impressive than the weight lifting "strongmen" he had known in his carnival days. "Casey and Germaine," he continued, "are not like those muscle bound cretins. As close friends, they are recognized as an awesome pair."

Hardrock blew a ring with his cigarette smoke, and added, "One time, Casey and Germaine were on a holiday weekend in Ketchikan, known as a wide open western town. They rented a hotel room and went out, looking for action. They drank a little and gambled some at one saloon, then moved on to another, and drank a little more. By this time their basic objective of the outing had assumed its rightful importance. Soon they succeeded in enticing a couple of the local ladies away from the other gamblers and carousers, and escorted them to their room to get better acquainted.

"I'm not sure how far things had progressed, but all of a sudden the door burst open and the boyfriends, or the pimps of the girls, plus a few friends, invaded. Our guys left the girls in bed and backed up to the closest wall. I guess the noise was about as loud as ice breaking in Glacier Bay. What with the shrill screams, loud cursing, crashing furniture, chair legs breaking and cries of pain.

"Pretty soon a couple of local policemen joined the gathering. By the time they arrived, it was quiet except for moans of a couple of the six guys on the floor who were not unconscious. Casey and Germaine were more than a little worse for the wear and tear, but still leaning, naked and wobbly-kneed against the wall.

The last reported words were by Donegal, 'Look what those bastards did to my knuckles!' "Well," Hardrock continued, " two or three of the invaders were carted off to the hospital for repairs, but fights and injuries are so common in Ketchikan, that no complaints were filed, or arrests made. However, the identities of two warriors who leveled six intruders were widely circulated by word of mouth, even though the report in the local paper left them nameless. "So it shouldn't surprise us to see that Casey and Germaine handle inanimate tasks here as well as the more lively ones in the city. Awesome they are."

CHAPTER SEVEN

Ole, Ole'

I wondered what was next. We had finished trap preparation, and Jack was to give me my new assignment. He knew I wanted to be a deckhand on the Cape Ulitka. Visiting the traps and helping deliver fish to the cannery was a very exciting prospect. But when I got to his office Jack said, "I know how you feel, but you'll have to settle for seeing lots of salmon in only one trap. We're a little short handed, so we need you to be a trap watchman for the next couple of weeks." I said, "Okay," and hoped my face didn't show my disappointment. He went on, "Your partner will be Ole Hemmingstead. Have you met him? He came in on the Oregonian."

I replied, "We shook hands as we were unloading the flour. That was it. His name sounds like Olee', how is it spelled?"

Jack chuckled, "No, it's just 'Ole'. It's funny with languages. The same spelling with a little feather mark over the 'e' is pronounced 'Olay." It's a shout of triumph to bullfighters." "Well, he's built like a bull, and seemed pretty solemn. Is he mean as a bull, too?" Jack hedged. "He was late getting here this year. I think there were some domestic troubles. He's always seemed serious, kind of a loner, but not unfriendly. He knows the ropes and should be a good teacher for you. You can win him over."

For the first time I felt apprehensive. Here it was, just after I had seen how strong these men were, and I was assigned to be with the meanest looking one twenty-four hours a day. His sour look reminded me of one of my Mom's favorite expressions, "He looks like he needs a good dose of Milk of Magnesia."

I kept reassuring myself that I'd be able to handle whatever came along. I bought the corked boots I would need to walk on wet logs, caught up with postponed laundry, and assembled borrowed reading material along with the books I had brought with me. Also, I pirated a few of Hardrock's crullers to help me through the transition.

The next morning Ole and I boarded the Cape for the two hour trip to the trap site. When we shook hands I was surprised that he had a fairly soft grip despite his obvious muscles. I hoped this meant he was going to take it easy on me. He was only about five foot nine, but his solid squared-off body must have hit at least two hundred five pounds. On a slightly smaller scale, he looked and moved like today's middle linebacker. His black hair was combed back away from equally dark, deep set eyes, like he was looking at you from a distance. He reminded me of the 1930's movie villain, Paul Muni, or Robert De Niro in his darker roles.

We didn't get much better acquainted on the trip. Eagerly, I renewed my comfortable relationship with Dan Starkweather, Al North, and the grumpy Sidney Smallstone, the crew of the Cape. So we hobnobbed on the bridge. Ole joined us some of the time, but said little and went below to the galley for coffee and smokes. I was both glad and worried about postponing our getting to know each other. I asked Dan if he knew why Ole seemed so withdrawn and unhappy. "I think he'd spent a couple of summers with an A and P cannery, and you probably know he's the brother of Carl, the cook on the Oregonian, who's lively and outgoing , a very different personality. But that's all I know. Well, you're always chipper. Should be good for him. But I wouldn't argue with him much."

I assured him, "agreeable" was my new middle name, but the pit of my stomach was not pacified.

Soon the trap was in sight and excitement suppressed my anxiety. Dan yelled, "Hey, Kelley, wait till we're tied up before you leave the boat." Here was a huge framework of flattened logs topped with a small shack. Over the door was a sign, "NEW ENGLAND FISH CO. TRAP #4." We moored at the front of the trap where the net pens, called spillers, were located.

From these the salmon would be dipped out, technically "brailed" into the tenders or their scows for the trip to the cannery. My pulse quickened at the thought of hundreds of fish tumbling and struggling to escape. But my heart beat slowed as the Cape pulled away, leaving me alone with a man I didn't know, nor want to know. I hoped

Chuck Reilly, watchman on nearby NEFCO trap, just like ours

his dour look came from unhappiness, not hostility. I forced back my fleeting vision of trying to share a cave with a hibernating bear.

The sight of our cabin heightened my anxiety. It was only ten feet square, perched right above one of the spillers. Surrounded by open sea and densely forested shore beyond the rocky beach, I quickly determined to take my chances with Ole, in this tiny floating home. There was nowhere to go. Was I imagining there was this tension between us? Maybe he was just reclusive. Whatever it was, it was going to be exaggerated by living in such a confined space, and he was clearly the top dog in our small sea-bound kennel.

It didn't take us very long to move in. Inside were upper and lower bunk beds, a two burner Coleman gas stove and overhead lamp, cupboard with kitchen equipment and canned foods, small table, two chairs, some shelves, a small wood/coal stove and a sink. There were also a few hooks and nails to hang clothes on, and a line we could stretch across overhead for drying clothes. Behind the cabin was a covered storage bin for wood and coal, a large barrel of fresh water, and a partly enclosed one-hole outhouse, with automatic tidal disposal system. There was also a twelve foot heavy wooden row boat, tied alongside.

Ole and I quickly agreed he'd take the bottom bunk and do most of the cooking, while I'd do K.P. Other aspects of living together we dealt with only out of necessity, as they emerged.

I did my best to keep out of his way, while he mostly ignored me, even when we bumped into each other. I was fully aware of the physical power he possessed. I was afraid of him, but almost totally dependent on his leadership. So, every time I had to seek his advice or direction I hoped he would be merciful. Gradually, he became somewhat more relaxed when he felt my acceptance of him as crew boss. Soon we set out on an inspection of the trap, which was exactly as I had envisioned from previous descriptions. This network of logs was anchored one thousand feet off shore, tethered to a thick steel cable, secured to a big steel peg imbedded in the rocks. The cable floated on planks like railroad ties, stapled across them every few feet.

Chicken wire fencing dropped from the cable to the sea bottom, guiding the migrating fish through a series of wire tunnels of decreasing size, until they ended up in the spiller pens of soft but strong netting.

Fortunately, Ole's Norwegian accent was quite easy to understand as he explained everything. By the time we made our way back to the spillers, it was clear that while the salmon could swim around and away from the trap, they were not smart enough to do so. We could see several hundred of them already gathered in the "pot," a wire holding area, until its tunnel to the spillers was to be opened the next day.

I had never seen salmon in the wild before. There were some fish that big I'd tried to catch in the Stillaguamish River. Later, I found out they were steelhead, with absolutely no interest in a dangled worm. Now, within arm's reach, were dozens of these slowly moving slender-bodied salmon. About two feet long and five pounds each, they seemed to move randomly while searching for a way out, and avoided contact with one another. Some of their sleek silver sides had dark streaks and arched backs.

"That's why they're called 'humpies'," Ole explained. "They change shape and color while they fill with eggs or sperm, as they head up rivers to spawn. They lay their stuff on gravel. Then they die."

I asked Ole about the long boards across the spillers, on the inboard side. They were similar to the plank I rode on my ill-fated gurry pot adventure, but these had hooks screwed into the outboard edges, every few inches. During brailling, Ole and I would be on our knees, facing the boat, and hanging the net on the hooks, forcing the fish up and away from us. As the net was emptied, boat crewmen would pull on ropes attached to the plank ends, moving it and us closer to the boat. If Ole and I succeeded in remaining on the plank as it slid, we would pull

Cannery tender, A.F. Rich empties its load of salmon into the hold. That's shirtless me walking the plank

the net up under the rest of the fish. Even the anticipation excited me. I could hardly wait!

By evening we had arrived at a reasonably balanced state of civility. Ole cut the belly fillets from one salmon, dipped them in cornmeal and fried them for supper. Served along with some canned vegetables, it was the first of our simple meals.

Our table was about the size of an ordinary card table, so we were pretty close together, even across from each other. I was mindful of the need to respect his authority, hence I ate quickly, eyes down, and carefully thanked him for cooking. No way did I want him to feel questioned or challenged. By the time I had cleaned up we were having innocuous short conversations about the food and supplies We even began our nightly games of cribbage. Ole was very deliberate in his play, while I, impatient, as well as quick with game strategy, realized slower pace was one of the keys to my survival with him. So I verbally counted out the runs, pairs and the "fifteens," instead of pegging the automatic total score of each hand. So far, so good. Amazingly, in spite of having so much to cope with, my mind slowed and I fell asleep quickly. Awake very early, I managed to descend from my bunk past Ole, who was snoring like the storied sawing of firewood. Still worried about how to get along with him, I crept to the doorway and slipped outside. A vapor veil of fog hovered over the trap, with magnified silence. Slight slaps of water rinsing the logs chirped like happy crickets. The planks floating the cable rocked like wing beats of migrating geese, disappearing in the haze as they stretched out to the shore. And the sea scent was saltier as it pushed up through the fog.

For those enchanted minutes I lived in my own universe, wondering about God, and wishing I was a poet.

Later, as the sun's breath slowly blew the fog away, the unusual warmth of the past three or four days revisited us. So, Ole and I set out in the rowboat to check all the floats and the cable. Everything was okay, so we rowed along the shoreline into a protected cove. Trailing my hand in the warmer shallow water I asked him if we should go swimming. His facial skin tightened, and he seemed to recoil.

"No, I don't know how to swim. I'd be scared..." his voice trailed.

"You can't swim?"

"Back home, no indoor pools. All water stays cold. Nobody swims, like in Seattle. Let's go back to the trap." Over time I discovered most of these courageous and strong men could not swim. They worked over the water in dangerous jobs, in spite of latent fear of drowning. I have never really understood this paradox.

By the end of our third day we seemed to be functioning pretty well, but still spoke sparingly. The spillers were now teeming with fish and we expected one of the tenders to show up the next day. I was really going to ride the plank and see all the salmon brailed out with big nets.

Ole, on the other hand, seemed especially edgy.

He sped up his pace while checking the spillers, then went back to check again. His short sentences became even more clipped, and his voice tone was barbed. I figured he must want to do well when the boat came. So did I, but I didn't have the same responsibility he did. I just wanted to stay on the plank this time, and not goof up.

That night, soon after we started our cribbage game, I held a sixteen point hand. As I pegged quickly in one move, forgetting to go slow, he burst into anger, accusing me of cheating. I tried to show him I hadn't cheated but his anger mounted. He leaned toward me, face reddened, and eyes fiery. "You're nothing but a damn little spy!"

Slowly, I backed my chair away toward the door, yet managed to reply firmly, "Whaddaya mean, spy?"

Shakily, he growled, "They don't trust me. You're here to make sure I don't sell the fish." He rose, hands squeezing, like eagle claws, body leaning toward me.

"I could kill you, boy, with my bare hands."

My whole body shook with the pounding of my heart. I knew he could strangle me, maybe tear me apart. I tensed, poised to kick him in the balls if he charged, then slowly backed into the doorway and somehow found the courage to respond.

"I know you could, but the second you touch me we both hit the water." It was only three feet away.

Ole straightened up. His eyes lost some of their fire as he assessed my resolve, and his fingers began to look less like killing talons. I was still very grim, retaining inner strength to stand up to him. My pulse slowed a little. In a standoff, we continued to glare at each other, but slowly began to lose intensity. Fear of the water tempered his anger, and fear of him slowly shook loose from my trembling body.

As we calmed, he appeared to believe my assurances. "I don't know of any distrust of you, Ole. I thought my assignment with you was part of learning. Jack told me that your arrival had been delayed because of some personal problems, so he thought it might be good for you to have somebody else to keep you company. That's it. I know nothing about selling fish." Actually, I had heard rumors of trap watchmen making midnight deals with fishermen, but not from Jack, or about Ole. His mouth tightened as he looked away. He seemed hurt and was silent for a moment, then, through pain and anger, told me what had been happening in his life. "I got married about five weeks ago. Ever since I've been trying to get it annulled or get divorced. I had dated this woman several times. She was a real tiger in bed. Then she tells me she's with child and I'm the father, cause she hasn't been with anyone else. She insisted we get married, and I wanted to do the honorable thing, like we do in Norway. So we found a justice who tied the knot.

"Well, that very same night she come sick with her monthly. So I knew I'd been set up. I was supposed to be here about six weeks ago. Instead I've been out of work and money, talking to lawyers, and wondering how I was such a dumb shit."

By this time I had stopped shaking, and actually felt sorry for him. I blurted out some false reassurance that everything would work out okay. After that most of the guardedness drained from our relationship. Ole and I never really became friends, but we were compatible part-ners. In our close quarters we still circled around one another, but out of respect, rather than suspicion.   I had parried and staved off the charge. I had passed another test. Ole, Ole

CHAPTER EIGHT

Keep Your Trap Shut

Salmon began to move in as soon as we opened the spiller tunnels. At first there were only one or two at a time. But soon, dozens, then hundreds of the shiny torpedo bodies were cruising the net walls searching for an exit. By reversing their route they could have sideswiped their incoming schoolmates and escaped, but none of them was smart enough to figure this out. Not so, with the seals which made their way in. When they spotted us, these sleek beautiful animals had no trouble finding their way back through the same tunnels. They were so stealthy we discovered them only when the trap exploded with frantic salmon trying to avoid being part of the seal's underwater banquet.

Ole and I wasted a few chunks of coal thrown at any furtive seal that stuck his head up for a moment. It was fun, if futile, but we succeeded in chasing him outside the trap, where the fish were only slightly less easy for him to overtake. One moment we would glimpse the black nose and dancing eyes among the thrashing fish, and the next minute he'd be laughing at us a couple of hundred feet away from the trap.

Even though I loved the excitement of the frenzied salmon, when a seal showed up, I became so protective of our fish that I vowed to bring my dad's 30-40 Krag rifle up next year, to shoot the marauding seals. Now, my view is completely opposite. Such an intention seems unnecessary and immoral, let alone illegal.

Sometimes there was a thrill even more special. We'd see a group of huge, graceful creatures swimming nearby. We called them blackfish, but actually, they were killer whales, named Orcas. They were twenty to thirty feet long, shaped like a slender football, with wide fan tails and prominent dorsal fins. They were black, with glimpses of white underbellies as they rolled. They got quite close to us when they dove to feed on the salmon outside of the trap. Ole said, "We needn't worry about seals when the blackfish are around. Salmon are lunch, seals are dinner to those guys."

I was in awe at their presence, but resented them as well. Like the seals, we considered them enemies, because they dined on our common quarry.

Most of the time it was peaceful. Only natural sounds of flying or swimming creatures broke the quietude of calm. Sometimes raindrops were wrung from low dark clouds, making pockmarks on the sea as they touched down. More rarely, when there was wind, the sea tipped its white caps to us as its waves applauded against the logs.

Now that we had our amicable truce, Ole and I compatibly shared chores, and cribbage or checker games.

His moods were easy to spot and skirt around, since he was neither subtle nor devious. He was a very private person, so a lot of potential tension was avoided when I went off on my own. I needed some solitude too. Emerging from adolescence, I loved being alone to analyze what was happening. I knew the tighter fit of my clothes was not all due to shrinkage, and my muscles began, as the body builders say, "to take on definition." More importantly, reddish fur had miraculously appeared in places where its absence had delighted my teasing schoolmates in the locker room, but humiliated me. Also my cheeks began to show similarly hopeful signs. Finally! Often I would walk, trot, almost dance along the logs, in my corked boots. With the aerating wear of the calks, plus the constant soaking, the logs smelled more and more like the complex beach than the salt water itself. Often, I took out our heavy rowboat to check the floats and the cable. Then I'd explore the beach area. I found special joy in the rowing, itself. It seemed as though I could actually feel my body strengthen, as well as stretch. Plus, I reveled in learning to handle the boat and oars skillfully. Somehow I sensed that I would need this competence later. Real confidence was creeping into my awareness. Maybe, I thought, I'm truly becoming a man.

Now we were at the height of the salmon run. The spillers filled so rapidly that almost daily one of the cannery tenders came to haul the salmon from the trap into the hold of the boat, or a fish scow towed alongside. This brailing was a lift out, swing over, and release process. As many as ten thousand fish were lifted from each of the two spillers. The boat's boom was swung across the stern, and a large round or rectangular dip net scooped out hundreds at a time and released the splashing writhing fish from their self-made cloud of flying scales and slime.

Ole and I worked well together as we rode the heavy wood plank that stretched across the side logs of the spiller, and was pulled gradually toward the boat. On our knees, we gathered the spiller netting and hung it over the hooks on the front edge of the plank, thereby tightening the netting, and forcing the remaining fish to bunch togeth-er forward. I thought it a fun challenge to stay on the mov-ing plank, slippery with fish slime, without holding on. It wouldn't have bothered me to fall in, except for listening to the probable catcalls, "The gurry pot kid's at it again." But Ole, with his fear of the water, grabbed the hooks and held on tight whenever the plank was being moved. As it turned out, we both made it through the season without getting dunked.

Each time we spotted one of our boats on the hori-zon I was excited and anxious. In my corked boots and oilskins I felt I was on a floating stage, with the damp mist curtain about to open, and the stage manager saying, "It's show time." Although the sea was usually calm, my tummy tossed and I sucked in a couple of extra-deep breaths of the briny air for relief.

Even the seasoned captains and crew members quickened their pace and sharpened their focus as the first dip lifted out the salmon. All hell broke loose! The frantic slaps of the fish against each other were like hundreds of rapidly clapping hands. Slimy silver flaked haze burst up and out. And the smell was concentrate of fish market. But gradually, as the spillers emptied, the players relaxed and shouted about the size of the catch, the numbers of the different types of salmon, and the progress of the run as a whole. Catch size didn't matter that much to me. I was too busy carrying out my work role, and sizing up the men. I'm sure the others, especially the skippers, were mentally converting the fish into cases of canned salmon, and dollars more in our paychecks. For me, the thrill of each experience was enough.

When the work was finished the skippers gave us our mail, which was delivered by boat weekly to the cannery. We also got other messages, and our food and supplies. Most times Ole and I were invited aboard for coffee and pastry. We would have liked to socialize longer, but the boats needed to get back to the cannery while the fish were still cool.

By the end of the first week the repeat performances were becoming routine. Ole and I were calmly preparing for the next boat, when the unbelievable happened. The right spiller erupted with a fish frenzy completely dominated by a blackfish in the middle. The salmon were frantically trying to escape, their thrashing sounding like a waterfall crashing onto the rocks below, and salt water spray was everywhere. A few fish exploded like silver rockets, over the logs into the target sea.

The whale was longer than the spiller, hence unable to build momentum, but any thrust put the whole spiller in jeopardy. The strong netting could not possibly hold this giant animal very long. It had to have entered through the narrow tunnel. If it tried to exit through the same opening the netting would be shredded, and the other spiller probably ripped, as well. So the entire catch might be lost.

Ole and I were powerless, and fearful for our own safety. But help was closing in.

By great good fortune, our biggest and best tender, the A.F. Rich, was coming in to brail. She pulled up to the front of the spiller holding the increasingly agitated whale, as it struggled to move around the surface of this cramped space. Elegant at a distance, It was awesomely frightening up close. About twenty-five feet long and at least four feet across, it's cavernous mouth seemed lined with rows of white tines. I froze in fear…no desire to be another Jonah. But the whale was afraid, too, as the boat arrived and the shouting men moved closer. This huge, powerful mammal turned outward, making pathetic, heart rending calls, sounding like a peacock's shrieks.

Ears other than ours heard the calls. Answering cries, ranging from similar anguish, to protective reassurance, to outright defiance, shot back from the rest of the whale pod milling around close at hand. We prayed they wouldn't try to leap over the log in a rescue attempt. Desperation and terror hovered over all of us, salmon, whales and men.

Quickly realizing that trying to lift the blackfish out would not only tear the dip net, but probably shatter the boom, boat captain, Carl Danielson, ordered a slip knot lasso made from 3/4 inch thick line. It wasn't easy, but the noose was slipped over the whale's flared tail, and tightened where it narrowed and fanned out from the body. In quick succession the boat was turned seaward, the engine set at full throttle, and the whale was pulled, white belly side up, over the slippery log. We didn't even have to cut her loose (Yes, it was obviously a lady whale). Her frenzied tail, flailing and writing on the log had frayed the line apart at the very moment she was freed.

She seemed uninjured, though her back and fin must have been scratched and bruised as she slid over the log. She was welcomed back by her pod mates, with joyful song and loud body hugs.

Amazingly, there was no significant damage to the netting. The tunnel was torn, but still functional, and we proceeded with the brailing, our pounding hearts slowly subsiding.

We all cheered when the whale was gone, and celebrated heartily when the job was finished. Modest Carl shrugged off the congratulations, but we all knew what might have happened without him. The whale had to be removed, dead or alive, before one or both spillers were torn open. The day's catch would be lost, as would that of each day following until repairs were completed. We were talking many thousands of dollars.

We had no champagne, or even beer, but the fresh pot of coffee and happy chatter were great. The guys said I was the luckiest kid in the world to see a blackfish inside a trap, in my very first year. This was rare. No one had even heard of this happening before.

Soon the season was over. Ole and I were all set to close up the cabin, and would be picked up in the morning. On the Cape's last visit I found out Jack Dempsey was keeping his word! The skipper, Dan Starkweather, called out, "Kelley, I've got bad news for you. You're going to be my deckhand for the next couple of weeks."

I pumped his outstretched hand, grinned, and replied, "Well, I guess I have to obey orders."

CHAPTER NINE

The Fortnight Legacy

The last evening on the trap. There was no breeze, no groundswell, no mobile creature. No work. Only still-ness…as though Mother Nature would savor our every move that night. One more special moment in this magic place. Now, a dragonfly glided gently west from shore, towing its elongated shadow into the disappearing sun. I thought, maybe we'll overtake him tomorrow on the way to the cannery . Then I smiled to myself, as I shook off my reverie of these days on the trap.

"My God," I said aloud, "we're outta here just when I finally got it figured out. What a couple of weeks!"

When we got here I knew from nothin', and was scared to death of Ole. We damn near came to blows. I stood my ground with courage I didn't know I had. Eventually Ole believed me, that I was no Benedict Arnold. Then the fish came in, and we brailed our butts off. Actually, we got raw fingers from pulling on the netting. The seals amused us, and that incredible blackfish in the spiller almost ended our season by herself. The boat crew guys said Ole and I made a good team, and Carl Danielson estimated we'd caught over 93,000 salmon, almost a record. Ole and I worked together well enough when we needed to, but went our separate ways much of the time.

Aloneness spawns both introspection and extro-spection. I sensed I was becoming a young adult and on my way to manhood, and the hours of free time nurtured this process. When I escaped from the tiny shack I was left to my own thoughts, and warded off cabin fever. I had walked, even run on the logs to keep my legs active. I had rowed all around, and explored the beaches.

I was surprised to find that I enjoyed solitude, espe-cially here. The sea amazed with its sights scrubbed clean each morning. Sounds were propelled wirelessly, the soft splash of a fish breaking water, a screech of a seagull overhead, or the call of a deer on shore, 1,000 feet away. Smells were salty, fishy and of wet seaweed com-post at low tide.

Soon I would be back with my peers, not just a "hanging around" kid. I've outgrown the Christian Science Young Peoples' group, which now seems too confining.. I'll take some ballroom dancing lessons, and muster up some courage in asking girls for dates. That prospect seems harder than taking on Ole. I'll seek career counsel-ing, get a job, and decide whether I should or could enter college next year, 1940. Plans for staying out of school this year had already been made. I wanted a year to catch up physically and socially.

The most meaningful of these alone times were those of reflection...of letting the universe come to me. While staying still, I seemed to enter a space of belonging, sharing nature's elements, being part of infinity. Cloudless nights were the most awesome. The sky glistened as though all the stars at home had reproduced. I wanted to reach up, pick a cluster of stars for Mom's hair, to bring sparkle to her side of the spotlight when she played accompaniment for show people. She'd be thrilled, of course, but probably too modest to wear them. So I only ran my fingers through the endless stars.

On this, another of those dazzling nights, I remember the one most overpowering. I awoke after midnight, went out to pee, and found myself on center stage in the Northern Lights Theater. The bath of moving colors must have hidden my nudity, cause I heard no snickers from the audience. Who would notice a slip of the brush in God's painting?

Amazingly, awareness of my insignificance in the limitless 'out there' fostered equal awareness of my significance here. However unimportant it is in the big scheme of things, my role is the one I have to work on, and the only one that I must play. If I have a calling, it has yet to be heard. Tomorrow I'll be a Cape Ulitka deckhand. I guess I'm ready to leave the trap and the cabin. Much within that cramped space goes with me. Much without that cramped space goes with me as well.

CHAPTER TEN

See Ya Next Year

With a familiar rush of excitement I tossed my gear over the rail and grabbed the friendly hands hauling me aboard the Cape Ulitka. A swift month had passed since my stomach had cartwheeled me from the dock in Ketchikan to the deck of the Cape, but my inside tingle was similar, in joining this crew as a deckhand.

Ole, noting my hurry, made a comment about not wanting to get run over, stepped aside until I finished my eager leap from the trap log. Then as the boat pulled away, we both turned and waved goodbye to the trap. We shook hands for a long moment. For an instant I felt like giving him a hug. But Noyes Island guys didn't hug, especially not this guy. But I suspected his eyes were as moist as mine.

Later, I wondered how I could have such feelings of warmth, even affection, for someone I didn't really like, and with whom I had nearly come to blows. I decided that a bond is formed when people live together in close quarters, a kinship kind of love grows out of their interdependence, even if they don't fully like each other.

Al took me on a quick review of the spaces below deck: the forward hatch, where the anchor chain and spare lines were stored; our sleeping quarters; the engine room; and the spacious cargo hold. There was marked contrast of smells between above and below deck. Topside had the clean fresh salty sea smell particularly while underway. Below were the odors of grease and oil, with hovering hints of a gym locker room. The bunks were small, and the mattresses thin. Actually, none of these aspects was a deterrent, but an earthy element in my ongoing adventure. Happily but anxious to fit in, I stowed my things on the top bunk above Al's. Noticing my nervousness, Al said softly, "Relax, Jerry, you're among friends." Fit in. Although only four years older than I, his quiet, friendly way had a fatherly quality, soothing my racing nerves with a balm of patience.

On the way back to the cannery, we tied up alongside a purse seine boat that had signaled it had a good catch of salmon for sale. Although the trapping season was closed, commercial fishing was allowed for the rest of July. Our tenders traveled to the fishing boats to buy and transfer the fish into their own holds, then head back to the cannery. The fishing crew could continue to fish. So here we were, alongside, stern to stern, hatch covers off, and fish flying, one at a time, from their hold into ours.

One of their men was standing thigh high among the dead salmon, throwing the fish with a fish pugh. This was a slender wood rod, something like a rake handle,

with a sharp curved steel point. In a smooth motion similar to throwing a shovel full of sand, or a fork full of hay,
one at a time the fish were pierced, lifted, and tossed into
our hold. There seemed to be little concern shown for
possible bruising or marring of the fish flesh.

Most of these salmon were called Humpies, for their

spawn induced humped backs, or pinks, for their meat color. They were more than 90% of the catch. Occasionally salmon called Kings or Chinooks, or those called Cohos or Silvers were caught. These were highly prized for their flavorful red meat, and their size. The Humpies averaged five pounds, but the Cohos ranged up to thirty, and the Kings up to seventy. Hence they were carefully pierced only in the head, or picked up by hand, for individual treatment at the cannery.

While the fishing crew took turns with the pugh, Dan and Al were tallying the numbers of the different varieties. Since the fishermen were paid a flat fee per fish, rather than by weight, each team kept count on mechanical tally devices. I don't recall the exact numbers, but even in 1939 a single set of the purse seine around a swarming school of salmon could yield hundreds of dollars. This was one of those times, so we left a very happy crew. Even as we got under way, they were preparing the nets for the next set, and one of the men was already on the bridge using binoculars to locate another school of salmon.

On the smooth run to the cannery I focused on getting better acquainted with my shipmates. Starkweather could have been the original "Dapper Dan." He was handsome, neat, outgoing and affable, yet somewhat distant. I figured this was part of the role of a captain, since I'd seen ' a similar reserve in Carl Danielson, on the Rich. Both of them kept their own counsel, and neither was "one of the boys." When I had a chance, I asked Al how Dan got the nickname "Fearless Dan," a snide term I'd heard used by the guys on the mooring scow, a few weeks before. Al looked around to be sure we were alone, chuckled, and chanted, "Fearless Dan. He's not afraid of work. He just lies down beside it, and goes to sleep."

I reflected a moment, realizing Dan often avoided handling the lines, or other typical physical tasks. That was how, compared with the rest of us, he always looked like he just stepped out of an L. L. Bean catalog. "Wow," I gasped, "If he's so lazy, how did he get to be a skipper?" "Don't fool yourself. He's a helluva boat man. He just doesn't like to get his hands dirty. If there's ever any trouble, he'll be there."

Then there was Sidney. Only a year or two older than I, he was about the same size, with scraggly blondish hair, and forgettable features, except for his pitted and neglected teeth. He followed orders, and worked well, but was uncommunicative and sullen. He was the only man in the place I felt superior to, so I either ignored him or tried to show him up. He was an easy target. While no etiquette monitor visited Noyes Island, most of the guys had a passing acquaintance with some of the common courtesies. Not so, with Sid, especially at the table. Protocol placed us at the end of the long table in the mess hall, hence, I couldn't avoid sitting near him. One night, when he was ready for dessert he called out, "Pie, Kelley."

I replied, "No thanks, Sid, I already have some," forcing him to ask me to pass the pie. Of course he didn't say "please," but his reddened face and the snickers around us were sadistically satisfying. By the time, several years later, I was appropriately ashamed, I no longer had an opportunity to apologize.

Within a few days I learned the basics of seaman-ship and dead reckoning, and was allowed to take a turn at the wheel without constant supervision. I was no longer in the way, and even Sid seemed to accept my presence without rancor. While towing a small scow alongside we would head out to the fishing grounds. We purchased fish that were unloaded into the scow, instead of our hold. Using the scow was advantageous. It was bigger, and a lot easier to clean. Besides, sometimes the crew at the cannery would do the cleanup. We could leave the scow, and be off on other business.

We were moored at the cannery each night. In the middle of one slumber I was awakened by the sound of metal clanging in the engine room about ten feet aft of my bunk. Someone was sticking the cranking rod into one of the holes in the big metal fly wheel that was turned to start the engine. By the time I jumped out of bed to see what was happening, the engine burst into life, and Dan was screaming down the ladder, "What the hell is going on?" Sid had also bounded out of bed. In a moment the three of us were peering into the engine room where Al was standing, back to us, with the cranking rod still in his hand.

Dan said, quietly, "Shut off the engine, Al, and go back to bed."

Al put the rod in its holder, shut off the engine, turned slowly, and walked past us to his bunk, eyes closed. Turned out that Dan knew Al was a sleep walker, and how to handle the situation.

When we kidded Al the next morning, he quipped, "I bet you thought 'somnambulist' was just another dirty cussword."

There were no other incidents like this that I know of, but a couple of times Al was probably starting on another one of "doze" missions, when he banged his head on the bottom of my bunk, and fell back into his.

We were now five weeks beyond the summer solstice. Twilight and darkness pushed the sun's rise and set phases toward their near hibernation at winter time. Morning mist was not sun steamed away, but cloud dragged into drizzle, then rain. Fishing was finishing, and the canning slowing, but the longshoring was at its peak. The cases of canned salmon weighed down the pier timbers, awaiting the Alaska Steamship Company freighters to assume the load. Hence, we, as the part-time, captive stevedores, were pressed into service whenever, and as long as each ship was there.

We loaded the forty pound cases onto sling boards, which were swung by the boom into the hold of the ship. We received our regular pay plus longshore wages for day work. At night, or on weekends we got time and a half or double time. Every four hours we had a one hour break and were provided with food. With the overtime, our earnings catapulted, a very satisfactory exchange for our sometime exhaustion. I was glad to work at a steady rhythmic pace, as I had learned earlier. And I was delighted to find I had much more endurance now.

The last days zoomed by, what with the sea and shore work both capturing what might have been free time. It was work, grab a few bites, and fall asleep in between, sometimes stretching out on a pile of the cardboard boxes. So I was a tired but happy lad when I met with Jack for the last time. I was to leave the next morning on the freighter now finishing loading. After a brief stop in Ketchikan, I would be in Seattle in three and a half days.

Jack congratulated me warmly, and added he was glad I had made it through the season. I said, "What do you mean?"

With twinkling eyes, but serious tone, he replied, "Well, after your little swim in the gurry pot, and a few other escapades, the guys put up a buck each in a pool predicting when you'd make your final and fatal mistake."

I stammered something about good luck, but cringed at the flashbacks of nearly falling off the pier while trying to chew tobacco, and almost being squashed between the boat and a piling, as I rinsed my hip boots by hanging over the side of the Cape.

"Geez," I said, "I'm sure glad nobody won."
Saying, "You might want to take this with you," Jack handed me a check for $847.00. This represented my earnings minus the small amount of my purchases at the company store. WOW! With all the overtime longshoring, this was my net for six weeks of hard work and adventure. In 1939 this was a bundle, more than enough to buy a new car. Later that autumn I was paid only $100 for six weeks

of warehouse work. And after expenses, my net was about $60, not including board and room, which my parents still provided.

I had made out like a bandit at Noyes Island. Wait till my folks see this, I thought. Maybe I'll buy Mom the new washing machine she's always wanted.

As we parted we shook hands, and actually hugged. Nobody was looking. Oh, he also gave me $33.00, and admonishingly said, "This is the pool money, but remember you still have to board the ship safely."

That evening I made the rounds to the mess hall, bunk house, and mooring scow to say so long. Almost everyone wished me well and hoped I'd return, but I was most touched by my buddy, Hardrock, who said, "Goodbye, Seagull. Remember to fly back."

I slept fitfully, dreaming of looking for lost coins, and rose early to have breakfast aboard the big ship. Leaving the crew of the Cape was not easy, even with Sidney. I wondered why it had been easier to leave my folks and Seattle, a few weeks ago. Also, I wondered how much I had changed, and what they would think of me now. Answers postponed, I hoisted my duffel bag, and climbed the gang plank to the waiting freighter.

As I found the right one of the four small staterooms, the ship got underway. I ran to the stern. When I leaned over the rail I waved wildly, hoping that would conceal my salty swallows. Though it was a clear morning my view was misty, as I watched Steamboat Bay and Noyes Island wash away in our wake.

The voyage was uneventful. As we lost latitude we gained a little daylight and the rain seemed slightly warmer. The inside passage was as beautiful south bound as north. There was little to do, so I caught up on lost sleep, read some current magazines, and contemplated what my future might hold. When the ship's doctor said "Okay," I stepped onto the combination scale. I had grown almost two inches, and gained twenty pounds! I now stood five foot eight and one hundred forty-five pounds. No wonder Jack had insisted I buy a new shirt and jeans before I left the island.

"Lookout girls, here I come! "

EPILOGUE

I returned my parents' waves and smiles as we docked in Seattle. They looked older and grayer, especially Mom, who never seemed to care much about cosmetic appearance. But they were both happy to see me, and I them. They exclaimed repeatedly about my growth.

When we got to my dad's pride, a 1939 Plymouth, he asked me if I would like to drive us home. I grabbed the keys, dashed around the car, and climbed behind the wheel. I was ecstatic. I headed south along the waterfront, toward West Seattle. Suddenly a west bound car turned left in front of us. I yelled, "Watch out , you son of a bitch."

After a moment of dead silence, my mother said, "Well, I guess he learned something up in Alaska."

***

Reaching For Manhood
At Steamboat Bay

Recollections of a boy's adventures in Southeastern Alaska

Summer 1939

Jerry Kelley